FUN FACTS

Ripley's
Believe It or Not!
Kids

& SILLY STORIES

HOP RIGHT IN!

Ripley
PUBLISHING
a Jim Pattison Company

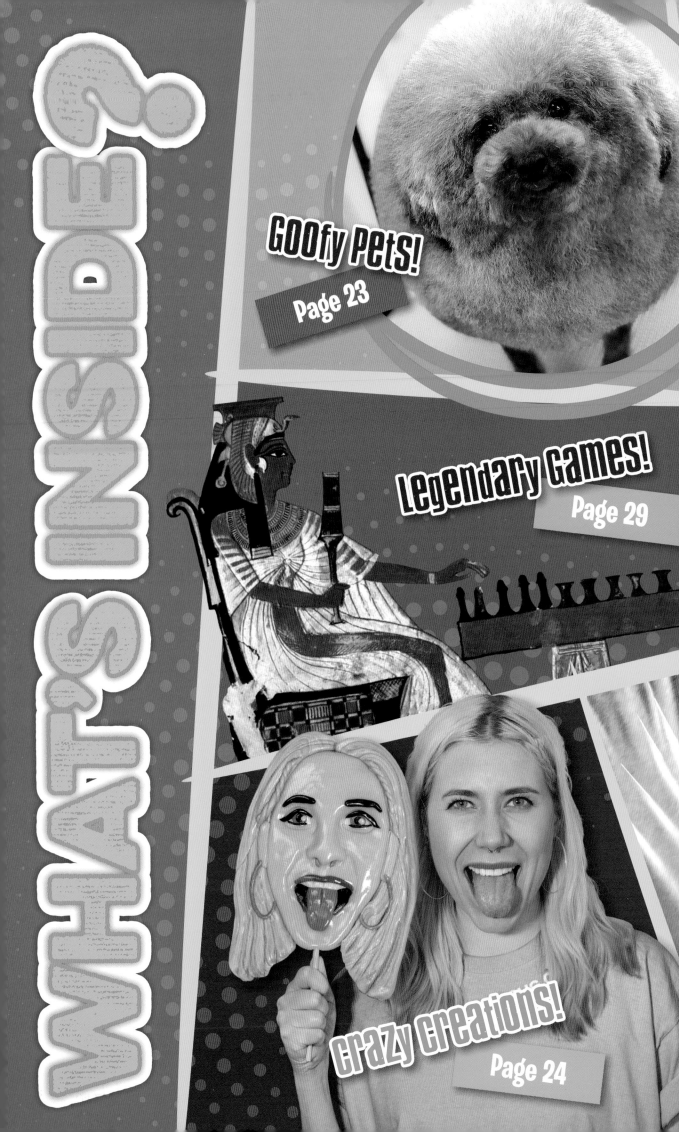

WHAT'S INSIDE?

GOOfy PetS!
Page 23

Legendary Games!
Page 29

Crazy Creations!
Page 24

FERRERO ROCHER

Check This Out!

HOT DOG!

Food stylist Erik Vernieuwe, from Antwerp, Belgium, uses wieners to recreate iconic pop culture images.

Some of his creations include Johannes Vermeer's painting *Girl with a Pearl Earring*, the flying bicycle scene from the movie *E.T.*, and Lynda Carter's TV superhero WonderWiener.

ANIMAL CROSSING

Mesh ladders were added to roadside drains in Warwickshire, Britain, to give frogs and toads an easy way out if they fall in.

Wildlife bridges like this one in Switzerland are used around the world to give animals a safe route over traffic.

Little blue penguins in Oamaru, New Zealand, use an underground tunnel to travel between the sea and their nests on land.

Christmas Island, Australia, has a bridge meant just for red crabs to safely cross the road.

Avengers! Assemble!

To promote the arrival of *Avengers: Infinity War* to Dubai in the United Arab Emirates, the Burj Khalifa, the tallest building in the world, was lit up with pictures of the characters.

Iantha Naicker of South Africa finished her drawing of Ant-Man with actual ants! She painted with the insects to entice the fruit juice to entice the insects into position, and then snapped a picture before letting them go.

UK YouTubers Colin Furze and James Brunton teamed up to build this 10-foot-tall build from the movie Hulkbuster: Age of Ultron. It can punch and throw flames! Avengers: suit up to suit movie

Superhero for a Day

Take turns with a friend asking for words to fill in the blanks in the story on the right. When you're done, read it out loud!

The other day, while I was _____ing at

_____, a _____ _____
      place   adjective   noun

came up to me and _____ed a magic
                          verb

_____ right in my face! All of a sudden, I could
      noun

_____ better than anyone in the world!
      verb

I decided to test out my new power by going to

_____ to see how I could help. There I saw
      place

_____ in need of _____, so I used
      person   noun

my superpower to _____ _____
                        adverb   verb

and give it to them. The next day, the headline of the

newspaper read: _____ SUPERHERO
                        adjective

_____S _____ : _____
      verb   adverb   noun

MORE _____ THAN EVER! Well, you can
          adjective

imagine how that made me feel. So I tried to

_____, but it looks like the powers lasted for
      verb

just 24 hours! Oh well, I'll always remember the day I

was known as The _____ing _____!
                        verb   noun

water WORKS

This fountain at a water park in Tenerife, Canary Islands, appears to float in midair! It's actually an illusion—the tap is held up by a pole hidden in the water.

On April 6, 2017, people gathered in Madrid, Spain, to cry together. Some people even used onions to get the tears flowing!

There are multiple types of tears!

About 70 percent of available freshwater is used to grow food and raise animals.

DOWN THE AISLE

In England, it's considered good luck to find a spider on your wedding dress!

In 2018, Vishal and Khushbu Agarwal of India set 6,690 diamonds into one ring!

In 2001, David Leibowitz and Kimberley Miller married 2.5 miles beneath the ocean aboard a mini-submarine resting on the bow of the *Titanic!*

Los Angeles artist Aaron Chervenak married his smartphone at a Las Vegas wedding chapel in May 2016.

In addition to being an artist and inventor, Leonardo Da Vinci was also a wedding planner!

It is legal to marry the deceased in France—dozens of posthumous marriages take place yearly!

When Queen Victoria married in 1840, she was given a 9-foot-wide wheel of cheese weighing half a ton!

On the Marquesas Islands of French Polynesia, it's customary for newlyweds to walk across their wedding guests, facedown on the ground, as they exit.

JELLY

CAKES

Siew Heng Boon of Australia creates 3D cakes out of jelly! She creates the see-through confections with floral patterns, wildlife, and even fish "swimming" through them.

Turkey Stampede

Oasis Camel Dairy of Romona, California, takes their turkeys to fairs across the state to have them race in a turkey stampede!

The turkeys follow a remote-controlled truck, filled with food, called "Big Red."

TURKEY STAMP

Want to see how you did? Turn to pages 88–90 for the solutions!

1   2   3   4   5

Follow the lines to find out which turkey reaches "Big Red" first!

LET iT

A 65-foot-tall snowman was one of 2,018 snowmen built in the city of Harbin, Heilongjiang Province, China, in January 2018. More than 3,500 cubic feet of snow was used to build it!

Between April 14 and 15, 1921, over 6 feet of snow fell within a 24-hour period in Silver Lake, Colorado.

SNOW

Snow is colorless!

Believe it or not, it can snow in the Sahara desert! More than a foot fell on the sand dunes outside of Ain Sefra, Algeria, in 2018.

Chionophobia is the intense fear of snow.

BARKING Mad

Spot, a 38-foot-tall Dalmation sculpture, carefully balances a taxi outside of Hassenfeld Children's Hospital on 34th Street in New York City.

Rachael Grylls of England and her dog, Jessica, can skip rope together an astonishing 59 times in one minute!

Dog groomer Yoriko Hamachiyo of Japan gave Sesame the poodle a perfectly round haircut!

You can mail a potato with your face on it through the Potato Parcel Company.

Spun Candy, a London-based candy shop, creates life-size lollipops of people's faces!

FACE!

Never lose your luggage again with Head Case—a fabric cover with a giant picture of your face on it that stretches over your suitcase!

Eat Up!

Get the best of both worlds with a sushi burger! The bun is sticky rice and inside is raw fish and vegetables.

A shop in Taiyuan, China, recently started offering vinegar-flavored ice cream!

A beach on the Canary Islands is covered in dead coral that looks like popcorn!

DagWoods serves up a unicorn-inspired glitter pizza at their restaurant in Santa Monica, California.

BOARD

It is theoretically possible to win Monopoly in just two turns.

Grab a friend and a different colored pen or pencil for each of you to play this game of Dots and Boxes!

Take turns drawing a line between two dots. The goal is to draw the most complete squares in your color—you can use your turn to block your friend from finishing a square!

GAMES

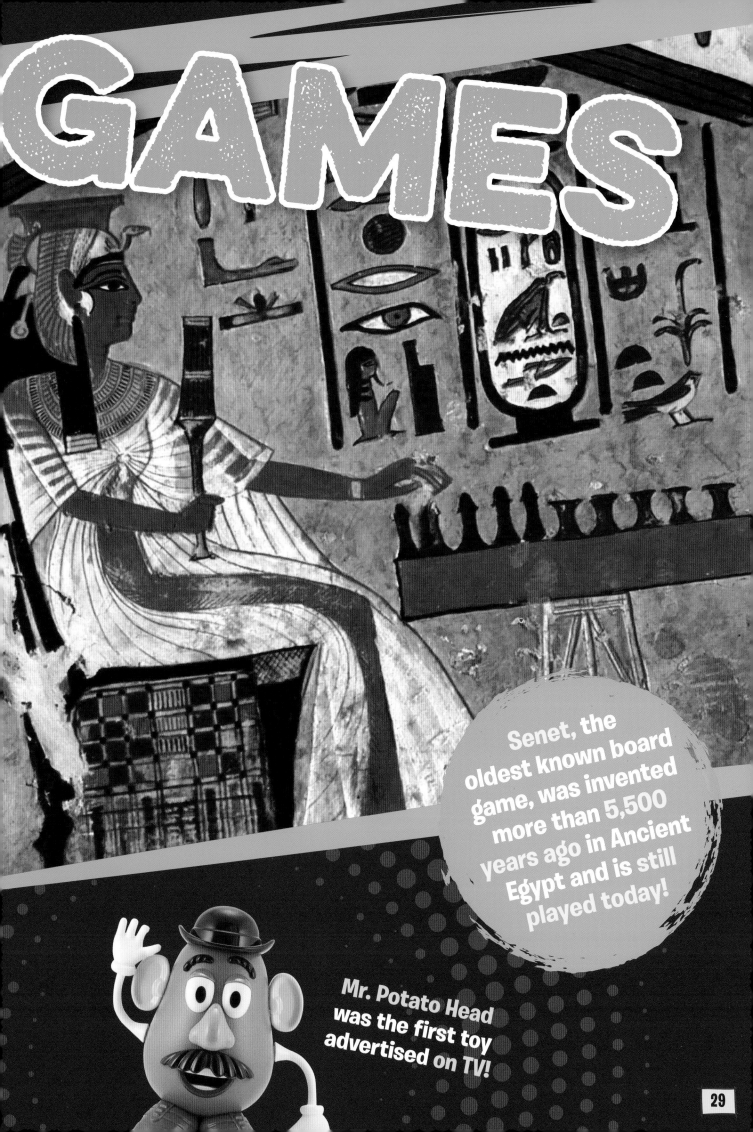

Senet, the oldest known board game, was invented more than 5,500 years ago in Ancient Egypt and is still played today!

Mr. Potato Head was the first toy advertised on TV!

OPEN WIDE

A gap between two teeth is called *diastema.*

Vikings carved grooves and patterns into their teeth.

The actress who played Violet in *Willy Wonka and the Chocolate Factory* wrapped filming with 13 cavities!

A hippo's lips are about two feet wide!

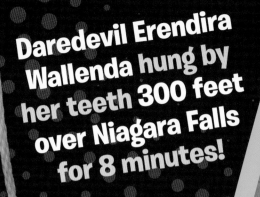

Daredevil Erendira Wallenda hung by her teeth 300 feet over Niagara Falls for 8 minutes!

Beavers have orange teeth!

Greek children throw their baby teeth onto the roof for good luck.

In the 1800s, some metal combinations used as cavity fillings would cause people's teeth to randomly explode!

CIRCLE OF LIFE

Photographer John Entwistle captured this rare supernumerary rainbow in Farmingdale, New Jersey. How many do you see?

This baboon in Zimbabwe appears to be using its baby to recreate a famous scene from *The Lion King.*

Technology company Vincross designed a robot that carries potted plants to sunshine.

RE

A giant purple sea monster took up residence at a former U.S. Navy shipyard in Philadelphia, Pennsylvania.

The inflatable beast consists of 20 tentacles, each between 32 and 40 ft long, and could be seen by people flying to or from Philadelphia International Airport!

LEASE the kraken

The piece, titled Sea Monsters HERE, was an art collaboration between Filthy Luker and Pedro Estrellas, plus the anonymous art collective Group X.

searching for

Can you find the mythical creatures hidden in the letters below? Make sure to look up, down, left, right, and diagonally!

```
C D J N N L Y B U N I C O R N
Q D R A G O N G C L F H Z Y Y
P F M B O C Q N G E C E T T L
G U L R F H G E V P N P J A M
M B X W A N R L A R T T R E B
E K N W W E I P R E D A A A H
R E N B P S F G Z C S X C U V
M Z W E P S F S P H I N X N R
A A S K X M I D Z A V O D B B
I U M F A O N I O U A K X I U
D H D A U N T H N N P R P G R
M C G I H S O K J S K A N F U
W L B R A T W T R O K K G O A
J E E V X E M F P M C E U O O
Y P S C C R J C X K I N W T X
```

DRAGON

BIGFOOT

CENTAUR

FAIRY

GRIFFIN

LEPRECHAUN

KRAKEN

SPHINX

LOCH NESS MONSTER

UNICORN

MERMAID

Want to see how you did?
Turn to pages 88–90 for the solutions!

36

legends

It's possible that legends of cyclopes (giants with one eye) came about when ancient Greeks found skulls of elephant-like prehistoric animals.

Can you see how early sailors thought creatures like manatees could be mermaids?

Dinosaur fossils may be why cultures around the world have dragons in their mythology.

Booking It

La Tête Carrée Library in Nice, France, doubles as a giant sculpture of a block head.

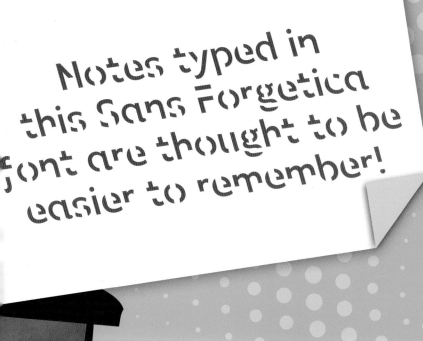

Notes typed in this Sans Forgetica font are thought to be easier to remember!

The Icelandic tradition of giving books at Christmas is called *Jolabokaflod,* or "Christmas Book Flood."

Uppercase letters are called such because printers used to store them in cases located higher than the "lower case" letters.

WHAT DO YOU SEE?

Pamela Warriner of Dover, Kent, was amused to find what looked like three smiling meerkats peeking out of her new fence.

mmer

Believe it or not, these rusty tools are actually chocolate! Treats like these can be found in chocolatiers across Europe.

Cranberries formed the shape of a heart while being harvested in Belarus. When farmers are ready to collect cranberries, they flood the field and ripe berries float to the top!

ROCKET MAN

YouTuber and inventor Colin Furze, of Lincolnshire, England, attached 1,000 fireworks to a bicycle—and then set them all off as he rode it!

He wore a special shield on his back to protect him from the heat of the explosions.

Elephant in the

British musician Paul Barton has been playing the piano for old, blind, and rescued elephants at Elephants World in Kanchanaburi, Thailand, for almost 10 years.

ROOM

African elephants' ears are shaped like Africa—a convenient coincidence that makes them easy to identify.

Elephants don't like peanuts.

Elephants can spend up to 18 hours a day eating!

An Apple A Day

Use these clues to unscramble the words, then order the numbered letters to reveal a secret message! The first and last letters have been provided for you.

There are more than 7,500 varieties of apples!

DARCROH

A farm where rows and rows of fruit trees are grown.

___ ___ ___ ___ ___ ___ ___
            6   15

DESE

You would plant this to grow an apple tree.

___ ___ ___ ___
4

REET

What an apple grows on.

___ ___ ___ ___
5   12

IPE

A popular type of dessert made with apples.

___ ___ ___
3

MOWR

Something you don't want to find inside your apple.

___ ___ ___ ___
14 9

The Big Apple structure in Colborne, Ontario, Canada, is 35 feet tall and is so large it could hold 653,800 real apples!

RAMLAEC

A sweet sauce for dipping apples into, especially in autumn.

__ __ __ __ __ __ __
10 13   7

LPEE

Some people don't like to eat this part of the apple.

__ __ __ __
   1

CERO

The middle part of the apple that holds the seeds.

__ __ __ __
   11   2

CERDI

A type of drink made with apple juice that can be served hot or cold.

__ __ __ __ __
      8

Want to see how you did? Turn to pages 88–90 for the solutions!

K __ __ __ __ __ __ __ __ __ __ __ __ __ __ __ Y!
  1 2 3 4 5 6 7 8 9 10 5 11 12 13 14 15

Snow Surfers

Surfers brave the cold in order to catch some waves off Norway's Lofoten Islands, located above the Arctic Circle, where temperatures can dip to about 9°F!

Some surfers stay after dark to enjoy the Northern Lights.

LEGO Wedding

In May 2018, LEGOLAND, in Windsor, England, unveiled an extravagant scene to celebrate the wedding of Prince Harry and Meghan Markle.

It includes the Windsor Castle, home of the British Royal family, made out of 39,960 LEGO bricks!

Even the Spice Girls, a '90s pop band, and Sir Elton John made an appearance!

MAD WOR

This chocolate couple were part of a "living statues" festival in Marche-en-Famenne, Belgium.

LD

The Bockenheimer Warte subway entrance in Frankfurt, Germany, looks like a train bursting up out of the ground!

The Cook Islands have triangular $2 coins!

HOP RiGHT iN!

Most frogs have teeth!

A species of frog on Borneo has no lungs!

The male Darwin's frog swallows eggs laid by the female and lets the tadpoles grow in his throat.

The fried bacon frog of North America is named as such because its croak sounds like it is saying "fried bacon!"

The southern cricket frog can jump to a height of 60 times its body length. That's like a person jumping the height of the Statue of Liberty!

In 1996, Kermit the Frog delivered the graduation speech at Southampton College, New York.

A frog in Australia was airlifted 500 miles for treatment after being accidentally run over by a lawn mower.

A species of fanged frog in the Indonesian rainforest is the first frog discovered to give birth to live tadpoles!

Help the lost flying fish find his faraway school!

start →

You found them!

Want to see how you did? Turn to pages 88–90 for the solutions!

FLYING FISH

Flying fish live in warm oceans. They reach speeds of 37 mph underwater before launching themselves out and gliding for as far 655 feet!

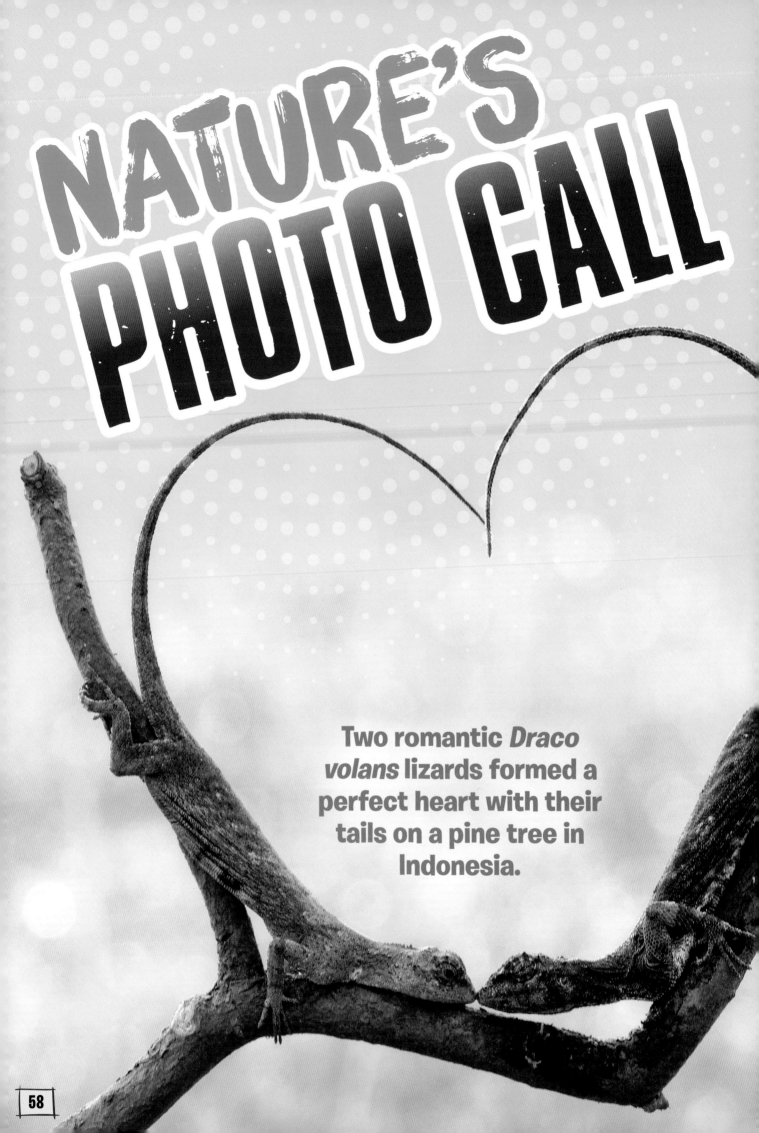

NATURE'S PHOTO CALL

Two romantic *Draco volans* lizards formed a perfect heart with their tails on a pine tree in Indonesia.

In Italy, a green mantis was snapped "riding a bicycle" when actually climbing up two stems.

A heron looks like it's sporting a thick mustache, but really it's eating a tasty frog!

SWEET Scul

Hong Kong artist Ciro Wai creates mini sculptures using the wrappers from Ferrero Rocher chocolates!

He uses his fingers, toothpicks, and pliers to shape the foil.

ptures

Some of his creations include mythical creatures, the Statue of Liberty, dinosaurs, and even Pikachu!

FERRERO ROCHER

FERRERO ROCHER

Banana Pops!

What You Will Need:
- 8 popsicle sticks
- Parchment or wax paper

Ingredients:
- 4 peeled bananas
- 1 cup chocolate chips
- 1 TBS coconut oil or shortening
- Optional topping ideas: chopped nuts, coconut flakes, sprinkles, crushed cereal

Directions:

1. Carefully cut the bananas in half; insert a popsicle stick into each half.
2. Place the bananas on a baking sheet lined with parchment/wax paper and freeze for 2 hours.
3. When bananas are done freezing, microwave the chocolate and coconut oil (or shortening) in a bowl together, removing every 10 seconds to stir until completely melted.
4. Dip the bananas into the chocolate and then any extra toppings.
5. Freeze for at least 30 minutes and then enjoy!

as!

Bananas are berries!

A banana tree's trunk is made of rolled-up leaves.

JOKESTER

Every year, clowns make a pilgrimage from the center of Mexico City, Mexico, to the Basilica of Guadalupe Church to give thanks to Our Lady of Guadalupe, an important symbol of Catholicism in Mexico.

Pilgrimage
(PILL-grum-age)
A journey, usually to a sacred place.

JOURNEY

FUNNY FACE

Design your own clown makeup! Will your character have a funny red nose? Or maybe a yellow bowtie? The possibilities are endless!

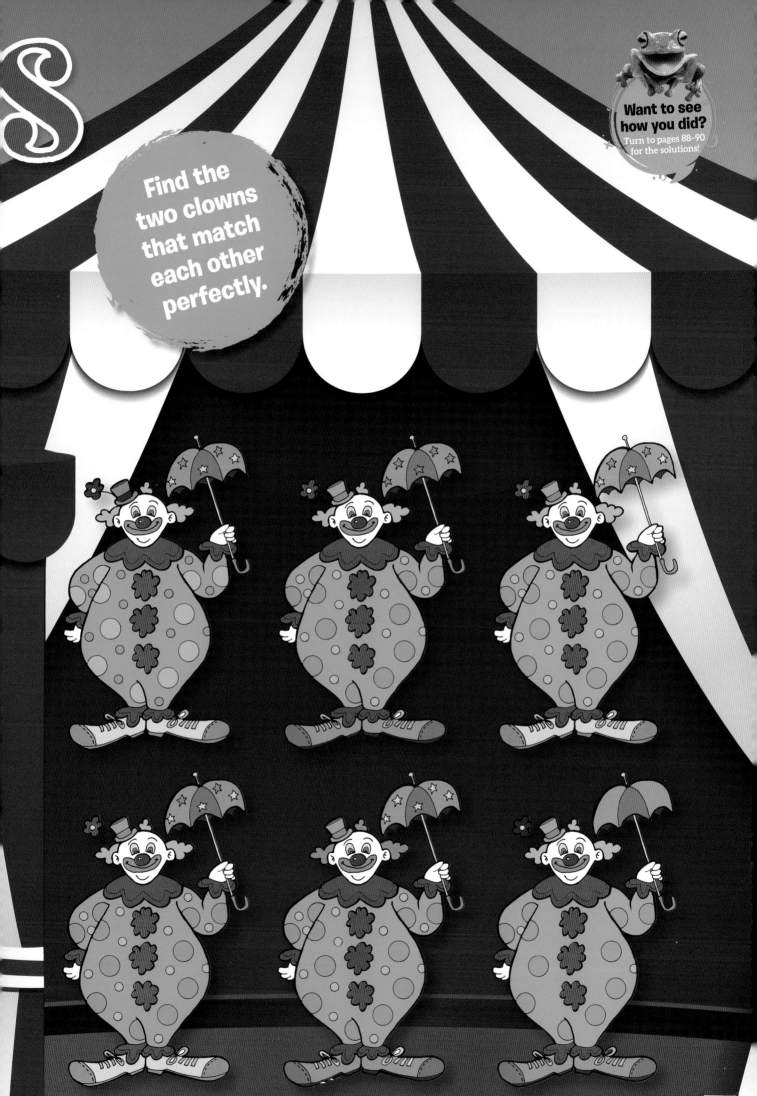

Find the two clowns that match each other perfectly.

HOTEL GODZILLA

Peering over the city of Tokyo, Japan, from the top of Hotel Gracery, is a nearly 40-foot-tall bust of Godzilla!

The movie monster can be seen not only from the street, but also from inside the hotel out of windows on the ninth floor.

SHIDAX KARA

One room inside the hotel is Godzilla-themed, complete with a man-sized version of the creature, movie posters, and a giant claw reaching through the wall.

FOX facts

They are one of just two members of the dog family that can climb trees.

You can find a fox on every continent except Antarctica.

Foxes can make more than 40 different sounds!

Foxes walk on their toes—it makes them extra stealthy!

Carefully fill in each square with the corresponding color to reveal the hidden image!

Want to see how you did? Turn to pages 88-90 for the solutions!

(1) (2) (3) (4)

Japan has bus stops shaped like fruit, instead of the regular garden variety.

RUCTION

It took about **10 million bricks** to construct the **Empire State Building!**

Cara Brookins, of Arkansas, and her four children used **YouTube tutorials** to **build a house** from the ground up!

A house in Nigeria was built in the shape of an airplane! Architect Jammal Said constructed it for his wife to commemorate her love for travel.

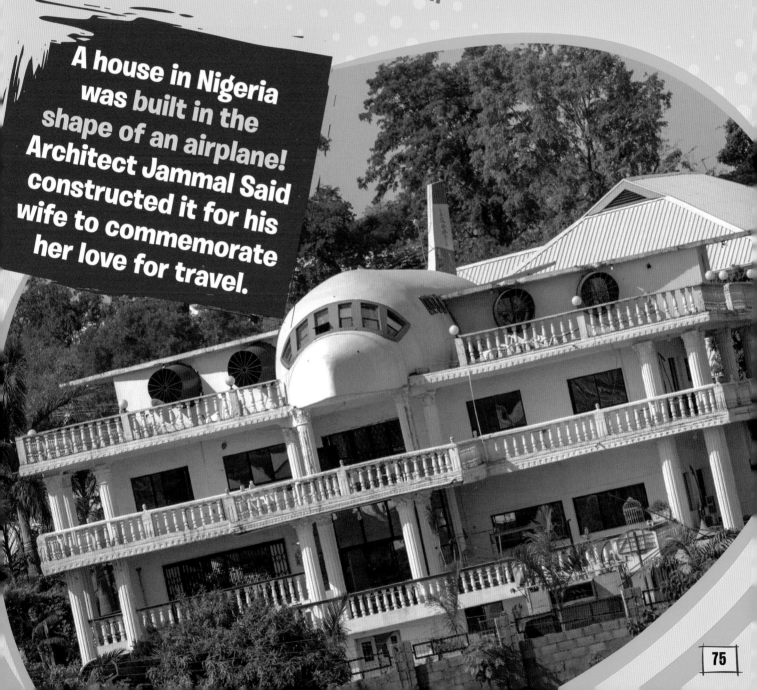

MASTERPIECE Match

Draw a line to match each artist to their famous painting!

Campbell's Soup Cans

The Starry Night

Andy Warhol

Frida Kahlo

The Weeping Woman

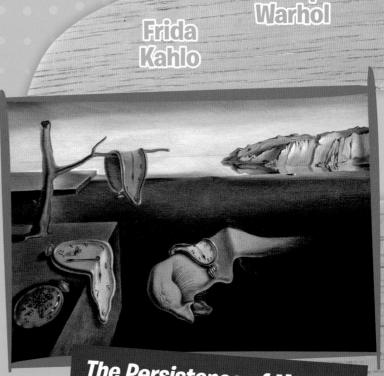

The Persistence of Memory

Mona Lisa

The Two Fridas

Katsushika
Hokusai

Johannes
Vermeer

Vincent
van Gogh

Leonardo
da Vinci

Salvador
Dalí

Pablo
Picasso

Girl with a Pearl Earring

Leonardo
da Vinci

**The Great Wave
off Kanagawa**

Want to see
how you did?
Turn to pages 88–90
for the solutions!

AWESOME ATHLET

Every year, Red Bull presents an event called Flugtag, or "flying day"—a competition in which people build human-powered contraptions to launch off a platform and into water!

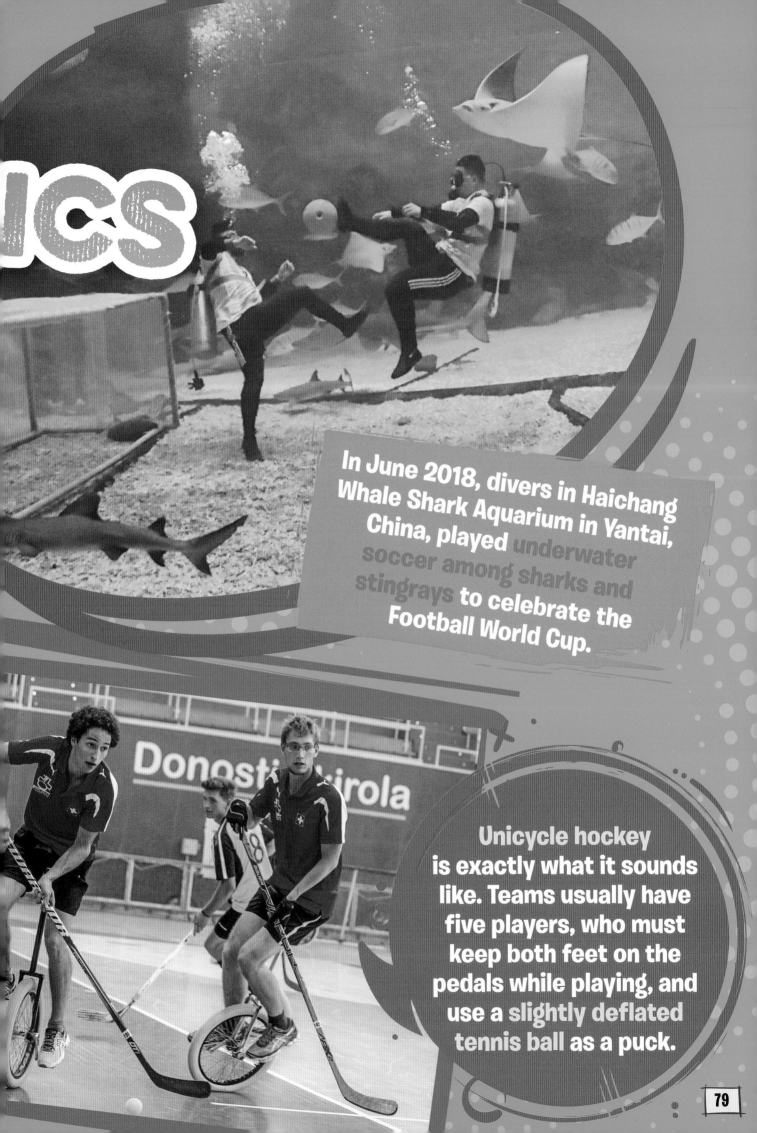

ICS

In June 2018, divers in Haichang Whale Shark Aquarium in Yantai, China, played underwater soccer among sharks and stingrays to celebrate the Football World Cup.

Unicycle hockey is exactly what it sounds like. Teams usually have five players, who must keep both feet on the pedals while playing, and use a slightly deflated tennis ball as a puck.

Holly Bridden of Salford, England, trimmed and dyed her dog Anna's fur to make her look like Woody from *Toy Story!*

A toy ship launched off the coast of Scotland in May 2017 by brothers Ollie and Harry Ferguson has journeyed nearly 3,000 miles across the Atlantic Ocean!

New York photographer Jared Middleton uses firecrackers, smoke bombs, and water to create realistic scenes with action figures.

A designer in Tokyo, Japan, built a Rubik's Cube that could *solve itself!*

See if you can spot all the differences between these toy boxes—there are 8 total!

Want to see how you did? Turn to pages 88–90 for the solutions!

FEELING

Visitors to Zhengzhou Zoo in central China can feed hungry koi carp with **baby bottles** attached to poles.

Shark babies are called pups.

FiSHY

The cylindrical saltwater aquarium inside the Aviapark shopping mall in Moscow, Russia, is almost 75 feet tall and holds nearly 2,500 fish!

GET

While cheetahs are normally solitary animals, this group, called "the Musketeers," hunt together in Africa's Masai Mara Reserve.

IN LINE

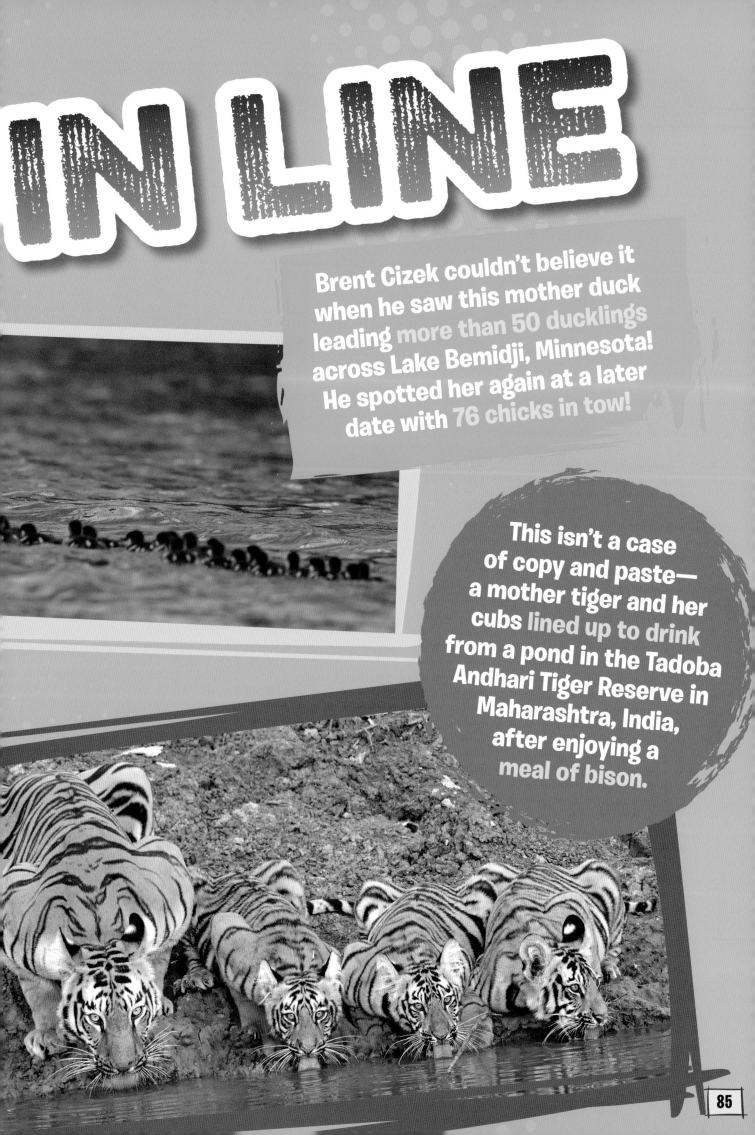

Brent Cizek couldn't believe it when he saw this mother duck leading **more than 50 ducklings** across Lake Bemidji, Minnesota! He spotted her again at a later date with **76 chicks in tow!**

This isn't a case of copy and paste— a mother tiger and her cubs **lined up to drink** from a pond in the Tadoba Andhari Tiger Reserve in Maharashtra, India, after enjoying a meal of bison.

SLIMY STARS

The walls of caves in Waitomo, New Zealand, are dotted with bioluminescent glowworms!

Bioluminescent

(Bi-oh-loo-men-eh-sent).
A word used to describe animals and plants that create light.

The glowworms use the light to confuse moths, which get trapped in the glowworms' sticky slime.

ANSWERS

SEARCHING FOR LEGENDS
Page 36

TURKEY STAMPEDE
Page 19

Word search grid:

```
C D J N N L Y B U N I C O R N
Q D R A G O N G C L F H Z Y Y
P F M B O C Q N G E C E T T L
G U L R F H E V P N P J A M
M B X W A N R L A R T T R E B
E K N W W E I P R E D A A A H
R E N B P S F G Z C S X C U V
M Z W E P S F I O U A O D B
A A S K X M D Z A V O D B U
I U M F A O I O U A K X I R
D H D A U N T H N N P A G U
M C G I H A S O K J S K N G O
W L B R Y A T W T R O K K N U
J E E V X E M F P M C E U O
Y P S C C R J C X K I N W T X
```

Words found: UNICORN, DRAGON, MERMAID, FAIRY, GRIFFIN, SPHINX, KRAKEN, BIGFOOT

A farm where rows and rows of fruit trees are grown.

O R C H A R D
      6   15

You would plant this to grow an apple tree.

S E E D
4

What an apple grows on.

T R E E
5   12

A popular type of dessert made with apples.

P I E
3

Something you don't want to find inside your apple.

W O R M
14 9

A sweet sauce for dipping apples into, especially in autumn.

C A R A M E L
10 13   7

Some people don't like to eat this part of the apple.

P E E L
1

The middle part of the apple that holds the seeds.

C O R E
11   2

A type of drink made with apple juice that can be served hot or cold.

C I D E R
8

SECRET MESSAGE:

K E E P S   T H E   D O C T O R   A W A Y!
1 2 3 4 5 6 7 8 9 10 5 11 12 13 14 15

AN APPLE A DAY
Page 46

FLYING FISH
Page 56

start →

You found them!

FUNNY FACES
Page 67

FOX FACTS
Page 71

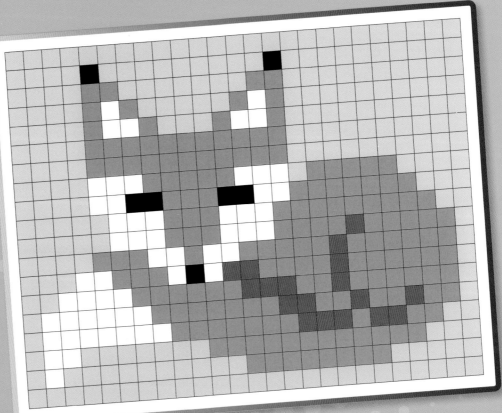

Campbell's Soup Cans — Andy Warhol

The Weeping Woman — Pablo Picasso

The Starry Night — Vincent van Gogh

The Persistence of Memory — Salvador Dalí

Mona Lisa — Leonardo da Vinci

The Great Wave off Kanagawa — Katsushika Hokusai

The Two Fridas — Frida Kahlo

Girl with a Pearl Earring — Johannes Vermeer

TOY STORIES
Page 81

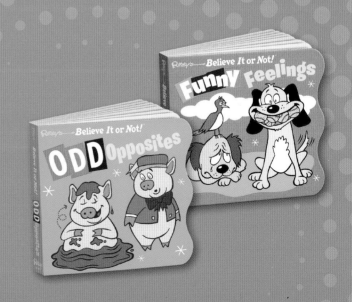

ACKNOWLEDGMENTS

Front and Back Cover (bkg) © Ornithopter/Shutterstock.com; **Front Cover** (b) © Kurit afshen/Shutterstock.com; **Back Cover** (t) © JoffreyM/Shutterstock.com, (b) © FotoYakov/Shutterstock.com; **1** © Kurit afshen/Shutterstock.com; **2** (tl) Yoriko Hamachiyo/Cover Images, (c) Public Domain [The Yorck Project (2002) 10.000 Meisterwerke der Malerei (DVD-ROM), distributed by DIRECTMEDIA Publishing GmbH. ISBN: 3936122202.] via Wikimedia, (bl) Firebox/Solent News/REX/Shutterstock; **3** (bl) Geoff Robinson Photography/REX/Shutterstock, (tl) Ciro Wai/Cover Images, (tr) © Sergey Rusakov/Shutterstock.com; **4-5** Burpzine/Caters; **6-7** © swissdrone/Shutterstock.com; **6** REUTERS; **7** Russ Bishop/Alamy Stock Photo; **8-9** Paul Brown/REX/Shutterstock; **8** IANTHA NAIKER/CATERS NEWS; **9** Geoff Robinson Photography/REX/Shutterstock; **10-11** © Rawpixel.com/Shutterstock.com; **12** mauritius images GmbH/Alamy Stock Photo; **13** (t) © Bakai/Shutterstock.com, (c) Marcos del Mazo/Alamy Stock Photo, (b) © bioraven/Shutterstock.com; **14** (t) © Nikodem Nijaki/Shutterstock.com, (cl) © Natykach Nataliia Shutterstock.com, (cr) © Blue Vista Design/Shutterstock.com, (b) © This Is Me/Shutterstock.com; **15** (tl) © Oleg Golovnev/Shutterstock.com, (tl) © Annie Leong/Shutterstock.com, (tl) © LiliGraphie/Shutterstock.com, (bl) © Rustle/Shutterstock.com, (tr) © Viktorija Reuta/Shutterstock.com, (cr) © Mega Pixel/Shutterstock.com, (br) © Anton Starikov/Shutterstock.com; **16-17** Jelly Alchemy/Caters News; **18** MARK RALSTON/AFP/Getty Images; **19** (bkg) © Veronica Lara/Shutterstock.com, © VOOK/Shutterstock.com; **20-21** © derdour rachid/Shutterstock.com; **20** ImagineChina; **21** ImagineChina; **22-23** Cover Images; **22** Richard Austin/REX/Shutterstock; **23** Yoriko Hamachiyo/Cover Images; **24** (tl) © Valentina Razumova/Shutterstock.com, (tl) © Vladimir Konstantinov/Shutterstock.com, (br) Firebox/Solent News/REX/Shutterstock; **25** Firebox/Solent News/REX/Shutterstock; **26** (t) © Isaphoto2016/Shutterstock.com, (b) Imaginechina; **27** DagWoods/Cover Images; **28** © Buturlimov Pavlo/Shutterstock.com; **29** (t) Public Domain [The Yorck Project (2002) 10.000 Meisterwerke der Malerei (DVD-ROM), distributed by DIRECTMEDIA Publishing GmbH. ISBN: 3936122202.] via Wikimedia, (b) © Nicescene/Shutterstock.com; **30** (tl) © sanneberg/Shutterstock.com, (tr) © WICHAI WONGJONGJAIHAN/Shutterstock.com, (bl) © Phawat/Shutterstock.com, (br) © Eric Isselee/Shutterstock.com; **31** (tl) © Perfect Lazybones/Shutterstock.com, (tr) © Sergey Rusakov/Shutterstock.com, (c) © Dmitry Guzhanin/Shutterstock.com, (br) © Julien Tromeur/Shutterstock.com; **32** JOHN ENTWISTLE/CATERS; **33** (tl) AF archive/Walt Disney/Alamy Stock Photo, (tr) Dafna Ben Nun/Caters News, (b) © osamuraisan/Shutterstock.com; **34-35** Group X/Cover Images; **36-37** (bkg) © Shutter Ryder/Shutterstock.com, © Pretty Vectors/Shutterstock.com; **37** (t) © Bernhard Richter/Shutterstock.com, (c) © vkilikov/Shutterstock.com; **38** © Anton_Ivanov/Shutterstock.com; **39** (b) © Nyvlt-art/Shutterstock.com; **40** (l) Bournemouth News/REX/Shutterstock, (r) © Anan Kaewkhammul/Shutterstock.com; **41** (t) © SunnyChinchilla/Shutterstock.com, (b) SERGEI GAPON/AFP/Getty Images; **42-43** Geoff Robinson Photography/REX/Shutterstock; **42** Geoff Robinson Photography/REX/Shutterstock; **43** Geoff Robinson Photography/REX/Shutterstock; **44** Paul Barton/Caters; **45** (tl) © Robert Biedermann/Shutterstock.com, (tr) © Patryk Kosmider/Shutterstock.com, (br) © Madlen/Shutterstock.com; **46** © topseller/Shutterstock.com; **47** © JHVEPhoto/Shutterstock.com; **48-49** OLIVIER MORIN/AFP/Getty Images; **49** (t) OLIVIER MORIN/AFP/Getty Images; **50** DANIEL LEAL-OLIVAS/AFP/Getty Images; **51** (t) DANIEL LEAL-OLIVAS/AFP/Getty Images, (c) DANIEL LEAL-OLIVAS/AFP/Getty Images, (b) DANIEL LEAL-OLIVAS/AFP/Getty Images; **52** REUTERS/Yves Herman; **53** (t) Stefano Paterna/Alamy Stock Photo, (b) © Thanakrit Homsiri/Shutterstock.com; **54** (t) © Don Mammoser/Shutterstock.com, (cl) © photosync/Shutterstock.com, (cr) © BlueRingMedia/Shutterstock.com, (bl) © Manfred Ruckszio/Shutterstock.com, (br) © Best_photo_studio/Shutterstock.com; **55** (l) © Luciano Mortula - LGM/Shutterstock.com, (tr) © Tinseltown/Shutterstock.com, (cr) © Talaj/Shutterstock.com, (br) © Menna/Shutterstock.com; **56** (bkg) © Proskurina Yuliya/Shutterstock.com, (c) © Haosame/Shutterstock.com, (tl) © Aleksei Martynov/Shutterstock.com, (tr) © Aleksei Martynov/Shutterstock.com, (br) © ridjam/Shutterstock.com; **57** robertharding/Alamy Stock Photo; **58-59** Ery Budi Nurhudha/Solent News/REX/Shutterstock; **59** (tr) Alberto Ghizzi Panizza/Solent News/Shutterstock, (br) Sherri Hendricks/Solent News/REX/Shutterstock; **60-61** (dp) Ciro Wai/Cover Images; **60** (tl) Ciro Wai/Cover Images; **61** (tr) Ciro Wai/Cover Images; **63** (t) © Maks Narodenko/Shutterstock.com, (c) © Ekaterina Markelova/Shutterstock.com, (b) © Cesare Cartoon/Shutterstock.com; **64-65** ALFREDO ESTRELLA/AFP/Getty Images; **65** Miguel Tovar/LatinContent/Getty Images; **66-67** (bkg) © Serafima82/Shutterstock.com; **68-69** Chris McGrath/Getty Images; **68** Chris McGrath/Getty Images; **69** John S Lander/LightRocket via Getty Images; **70** (t) © Geoffrey Kuchera/Shutterstock.com, (bl) © LuckyVector/Shutterstock.com; **71** (t) © EvgenyPlotnikov/Shutterstock.com, (b) © Kalinicheva Mariia/Shutterstock.com; **72** (tl) Rodney Nombekana/Caters News, (b) MATTHEW TOLZMANN/Caters News; **73** (t) Grahm S. Jones/Caters News, (b) MATTHEW TOLZMANN/Caters News; **74** (t) John S Lander/LightRocket via Getty Images, (b) John S Lander/LightRocket via Getty Images; **75** (tl) Icon made by Bogdan Rosu from www.flaticon.com, (tr) Icon made by Freepik from www.flaticon.com, (b) REUTERS/Goran Tomasevic; **76-77** (bkg) © Africa Studio/Shutterstock.com; **76** (tl) Peter Barritt/Alamy Stock Photo, (tr) Public Domain [bgEuwDxel93-Pg at Google Cultural Institute] via Wikimedia, (bl) Guillem Lopez/Alamy Stock Photo, (br) Peter Horree/Alamy Stock Photo; **77** (tl) Public Domain [Musée du Louvre] via Wikimedia, (tr) Archivart/Alamy Stock Photo, (bl) Public Domain [Library of Congress] via Wikimedia, (br) Public Domain [www.geheugenvannederland.nl] via Wikimedia; **78** VASILY MAXIMOV/AFP/Getty Images; **79** (t) VCG/VCG via Getty Images, (r) GARI GARAIALDE/AFP/Getty Images; **80** (t) MERCURY PRESS via Caters News, (c) © Businessvector/Shutterstock.com, (b) Jared Middleton/Caters News; **81** (tr) © rcherem/Shutterstock.com; **82** (t) ImagineChina; **83** © Julia Kuznetsova/Shutterstock.com; **84-85** BRENT CIZEK/CATERS; **84** Christopher Misztur/Solent News/REX/Shutterstock; **85** Tanay Panpalia/Solent News/REX/Shutterstock; **87-88** Shaun Jeffers/Caters News; **87** CATERS NEWS; **91** © Ton Bangkeaw/Shutterstock.com; **93** © Kurit afshen/Shutterstock.com; **Master Graphics** © Shmelkova Nataliya/Shutterstock.com, © phipatbig/Shutterstock.com, © Milan M/Shutterstock.com, © StarLine/Shutterstock.com, © Kurit afshen/Shutterstock.com, © Chinch/Shutterstock.com

Key: t = top, b = bottom, c = center, l = left, r = right, sp = single page, bkg = background
All other photos are from Ripley Entertainment Inc.

Every attempt has been made to acknowledge correctly and contact copyright holders, and we apologize in advance for any unintentional errors or omissions, which will be corrected in future editions.